This The Wonder Boy's Goldfish book belongs to :

____

____

____

To all children worldwide,
you are wonderful, you are amazing,
you are loved!

The wonder boy's goldfish is an amazing book suitable for kids of all ages. It revolves around a major character; wonder boy and it is written in a simple way for children to read and understand.

The book can be read independently by children who are learning to read confidently and also be used as a study aid.

Children reading this book should learn about deforestation and it's impact, with major focus on wild life conservation, flooding and global warming.

The wonder boy's goldfish book is carefully structured to include vital words that would enhance children's reading and comprehension abilities.

The text on each pages are closely supported by scenes and props that help with understanding of the message been put across in the text.

Children should be asked what they understand from each illustration and given the chance to retell the story after each reading session.

Let children look through the pictures and study the moral lessons from the book, which is available on the last page.

The Wonder Boy's Goldfish

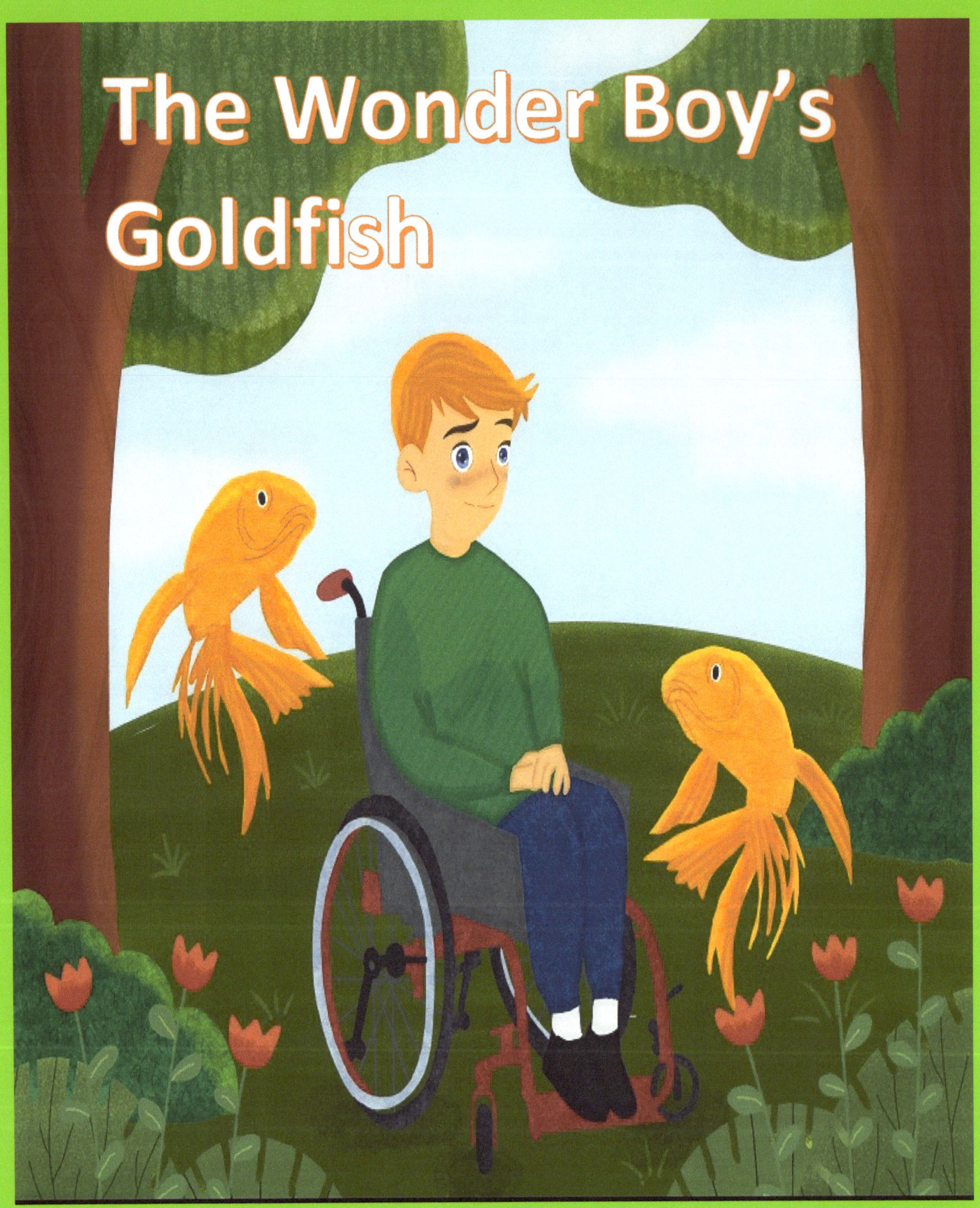

Born special and living in a tree top house, wonder boy was a happy child.

His mummy and daddy loved him very much.

Wonder boy liked to play games on
his mummy's mobile phone.
He also loved going outdoors to play
with his friends.

Wonder boy had a brother and a
sister.
They loved him very much.

Wonder boy could not walk on land,
but he could walk in water.
He had magical powers !
He played in the water like a
dolphin.

Oh, he was indeed special and
amazing!

One day, his mummy bought him a
goldfish.
Wonder boy called her Daisy.

Wonder boy loved Daisy the goldfish
so much, she slept in a plastic
aquarium close to his bed.

Daisy the goldfish ate fish food and
her best friend was wonder boy.

Wonder boy was born special.

He was created to get extra love and care from his friends and family.

His mummy and daddy didn't know
wonder boy was created special,
until he was 10 months old.

One day some loggers went to
wonder boy's home to cut down the
tree house where he lived with his
family.

They cut down the tree house and made wonder boy and his family homeless.
Daisy the goldfish was very sad.

Suddenly it began to rain, then
came the flood.
Wonder boy and his family were
stranded.
Daisy the goldfish ran into the sea
to get help.

She told the sea creatures what had
happened to her best friend's
family.

Daisy the goldfish led the sea creatures to rescue her best friend's family.

The sea creatures built a bridge
to rescue wonder boy and his
family from the flood.

The family was grateful to Daisy the goldfish and her friends, for saving them. They said "thank you" to the sea creatures.

Wonder boy's family built a new
house and they lived happily
again.

Words to practice and their meaning

Afforestation   *planting forest trees in an area with no trees*
Aquarium   *a transparent tank of water which live fish are kept*
Bridge   *a structure creating a pathway across a river*

Created   *to bring something into existence*

Diagnosis   *to identify the nature of an illness*
Deforestation   *clearing a wide area of trees*
Extra   *added to the usual amount or number*
Fish Food   *plant based material used to feed fish*
Flood   *an overflow of a large amount of water beyond it's normal limits*
Goldfish   *a small usually golden-orange Asian cyprinid fish*
Grateful   *showing appreciation for something received*

Loggers   *a person who cut down trees, may also be called a lumberjack*
Rescue   *to help someone out of a difficult situation*
Sea creatures   *animals that live in the sea*

Special   *being different from what is usual*

Stranded   *not being able to move from somewhere*

Suddenly   *when something happen quickly or unexpectedly*

Moral Lessons From The Wonder Boy's Goldfish Book.

Love yourself and love your friends, everyone will be happy.

People with disabilities have untapped abilities, they should be given
   extra love and care.

The forest is a very important part of our life, we should protect
   the forest.

Unauthorized logging can make people and animals sad and
loose their homes.

Animals have feelings just like humans, we should love
   and protect our pets.

March 21 is international day of the forest.

How much do you remember from the wonder boy's goldfish book?
Answer these questions and find out !

At what age did wonder boy's family find
out he was a special child?

What did wonder boy liked doing ?

Did wonder boy have any siblings?

Why did wonder boy and his family become homeless?

How did wonder boy's goldfish rescue the family?

Who are the main characters in the story?

What did you learn from the wonder boy's story?

Look at the pictures from the story and rearrange them in the right order.